Y0-DWI-022

RAPTORS

FALCONS

JULIE K. LUNDGREN

ROURKE PUBLISHING

Vero Beach, Florida 32964

www.rourkepublishing.com

Project Assistance:
The author also thanks raptor specialist Frank Taylor and the team at Blue Door Publishing.

Photo credits: Cover © Holly Kuchera; Title Page © Brooke Whatnall; Contents Page © Holly Kuchera; Page 4 © Frank Taylor; Page 5 © EcoPrint; Page 6 © Daniel Hebert; Page 7 © Dennis Donohue; Page 8 © Dennis Donohue; Page 9 © 2399; Page 10 © Kevin L. Cole; Page 11 © landbysea; Page 12 © Bodil1955; Page 13 © Rui Saraiva; Page 14 © Bufo, sgaorishal; Page 16 © US Fish & Wildlife; Page 17 © Tyler Olson; Page 18 © Frank Taylor; Page 19 © Kenneth Sponsler; Page 20 © www.naturespicsonline.com; Page 21 © Rikard Stadler; Page 22 © Oleg Kozlov, Sophy Kozlova;

Editor: Meg Greve

Cover and page design by Nicola Stratford, Blue Door Publishing

Library of Congress Cataloging-in-Publication Data

Lundgren, Julie K.
  Falcons / Julie K. Lundgren.
     p. cm. -- (Raptors)
  Includes index.
  ISBN 978-1-60694-398-4 (hard cover)
  ISBN 978-1-60694-776-0 (soft cover)
  1. Falcons--Juvenile literature. 1. Title.
  QL696.F34L86 2010
  598.9'6--dc22
                                              2009000534

Printed in the USA
CG/CG

www.rourkepublishing.com - rourke@rourkepublishing.com
Post Office Box 643328 Vero Beach, Florida 32964

Contents

Speed Demons

Birds of **prey**, or raptors, catch and eat other animals. Falcons, a kind of raptor, have pointed wings and strong flying abilities. Their sharp eyesight and fast flying make them fierce hunters.

Falcon faces often have a stripe under each eye. Little brows, or hoods, shade falcon eyes. These two features reduce the Sun's glare.

4

Lanner falcons, of northern Africa, most often hunt quail, pigeons, and doves, but will also eat insects, lizards, bats, and scorpions.

Over 60 different kinds of falcons exist. Small falcons may eat insects, lizards, mice, and songbirds. Larger falcons can handle prey like pheasants and rabbits.

Some male and female falcons look different. American kestrel males have blue and red feathers, while females have brown feathers. Female falcons weigh more than males.

RAPTOR REPORT

African pygmy falcons measure about 8 inches (20 centimeters) long. They hunt for insects, lizards, and small birds in dry, open areas with a few trees for perching.

SECRET WEAPONS

Falcons have strong, hooked beaks to tear meat and sharp **talons** to grip their prey. Their beaks have a little sharp bump on each side called a tooth. Falcons use them to break the neck of their prey.

Gyrfalcons are the largest falcons. Their wings measure four feet (1.2 meters) from end to end. Gyrfalcons weigh 2 to 4.5 pounds (1 to 2 kilograms) and live in northern **habitats**.

Peregrine falcons most often hunt other birds. Their diet includes pheasants, doves, jays, blackbirds, ducks, and shorebirds.

Some scientists have put tiny video cameras on peregrine falcons to study how falcons hunt. Video watchers get a wild ride!

When a peregrine falcon spies prey below, it tucks its wings to its body and dives. It steers with its tail. A falcon's tail can make tiny adjustments in any direction for perfect control.

Diving peregrine falcons reach speeds of 150 to 200 miles per hour (240 to 320 kilometers per hour), making them the fastest animals on Earth.

Peregrines slash prey out of the sky, and then drop down for the kill.

American kestrels have the ability to fly in place while hunting. Once their eyes lock onto prey, they drop. Favorite meals include mice and large insects.

American kestrels have one more secret weapon. Their eyes can see a kind of light called **ultraviolet light**. Voles, a favorite food, leave a trail of **urine** wherever they go. Their urine glows with ultraviolet light. Kestrels follow the trail to their next dinner.

Hovering takes a lot of energy. Kestrels more often hunt from perches.

Kestrels and other birds of prey help limit the populations of voles, mice, and other small rodents.

Merlins nest in trees and on the ground. Each egg in this soft, grassy nest measures about 1.5 inches (4 centimeters) long.

Nests on High

Different kinds of falcons use different kinds of nests. American kestrels choose holes in trees. Other falcons take over old nests from other raptors or crows. Gyrfalcons, peregrines, and prairie falcons like high cliff ledges.

The number of eggs laid depends on the kind of falcon. Falcons lay one to five eggs each year. In a little over a month, the eggs hatch. Females often keep the young warm and under protection while males bring back food. Falcons do not build their own nests.

Young falcons need to eat often. Their parents feed them until they learn how to catch their own prey.

Once the chicks grow in strength and size, both parents bring food to their hungry young.

Peregrine falcons often nest on cliff ledges. In cities, they will nest on high bridges and tall buildings.

An open mouth and lots of squawking signal to the parent to feed the chick.

Falcons On The Fist

In the sport of falconry, a person, or falconer, trains a young bird to share the job of hunting. In the field, falconers walk along and scare up prey for the bird to chase. After hunting, the bird returns. The partnership allows birds to perfect their hunting skills without the dangers of the wild.

Once only a sport of royalty, falconers today come from all backgrounds. Many falconers prize gyrfalcons above all others.

Falconers get special training to work with a bird of prey. The falconer often frees the bird in a few years, once it has more experience.

Eyes On The Skies

Habitat loss, shootings, power lines, and **pesticides** threaten falcons. People work to teach others about falcons. Scientists and wildlife doctors think of ways to help falcons in trouble.

Scientists consider aplomado falcons **endangered**. They have started a program to help them. They raise young birds and release them into safe habitats.

RAPTOR REPORT

Falcons that perch on power poles or towers risk a zap of electricity if they touch an unprotected wire. Better power line design can help stop this killer.

See and learn about falcons and other birds of prey at zoos, nature centers, and in the skies. Know the facts to make sure we will always be able to hear the cry of the falcon.

LOSSARY

endangered (en-DAYN-jurd): at risk of becoming extinct

gyrfalcons (JEER-fal-kuhnz): the largest falcons, nesting in cold northern areas

habitats (HAB-uh-tats): the places where animals make their homes

pesticides (PESS-tuh-sides): chemicals that kill insects and other pests, especially those that eat farm crops

prey (PRAY): the animals that other animals hunt for food

talons (TAL-uhnz): a raptor's sharp claws

ultraviolet light (uhl-truh-VYE-uh-lit LITE): a kind of light from the Sun that cannot be seen by people

urine (YER-in): liquid waste that people and animals pass from their bodies

Index

Websites to Visit

Soar over to your local library to learn more about falcons and other raptors. Hunt down the following websites:

http://animaldiversityweb.ummz.umich.edu/site/index.html
www.peregrinefund.org
www.raptor.cvm.umn.edu/
www.hawkandowl.org
www.hawkmountain.org

About The Author

Julie K. Lundgren grew up near Lake Superior where she reveled in mucking about in the woods, picking berries, and expanding her rock collection. Her interest in nature led her to a degree in biology and eight years of volunteer work at The Raptor Center at the University of Minnesota. She currently lives in Minnesota with her husband and two sons.

24

DATE DUE